Objective Myopia

Copyright © 2020 by Marionito C. Marquez.

All rights reserved. No part of this book may be reproduced, stored in a retrieval system, or transmitted in any form or by any means, electronic, mechanical, photocopying, recording, scanning, or otherwise, except as permitted.

This book may not be lent, resold, hired out or otherwise disposed of by way of trade in any form of binding or cover other than that in which it is published without the prior consent of the author or publisher.

References to the websites (URLs) were accurate at the time of the writing. Neither the author nor the publisher is responsible for URLs that may have expired or changed since the manuscript was prepared.

Objective Myopia

ISBN- 9798686028937

First Printing

Library of Congress Cataloging-in-Publication Data has been applied for.

Objective Myopia

Why executives fail to secure the creation of maximum shareholder value and sustainable profitability.

By Marionito Marquez

What is the *One Best Way* to do work or to manage a business to secure the creation of maximum shareholder value and sustainable profitability in the passage of time and change in the economic environment?

It is a century-old question but one that we should all ask and answer before our companies fail, stop growing, or may end up being sold for survival. Many executives who achieved the creation of significant amount of shareholder value and profit for many decades in the past did not ask or answer this question and the business organizations they run on behalf of its shareholders soon failed to secure the creation of maximum shareholder value and sustainable profitability. Why?

From the study and analysis of the history of wealth creation and the development of numerous transformative products, services, and methods to do work or to manage a business, we can find and conclude that many business organizations that achieved the creation of significant amount of shareholder value and profit for many decades in the past soon failed, stopped growing, or were sold for survival not because of lack of capital to enter in emerging business or because of the absence of economic opportunities to grow rather there was a failure from its management, primarily in the allocation of capital, due to its executives' own objective myopia.

A Century of search to find the 'One Best Way' to do work

More than hundred years ago Frederick W. Taylor, known as the father of Scientific Management, searched to find the *'One Best Way'* to do work or to manage a business to secure the creation of *maximum and permanent prosperity*. He stated in his own words

*"the principal object of management should be to secure the **maximum prosperity** for the employer coupled with the maximum prosperity for each employee. The words maximum prosperity are used, in their broad sense, to mean not only large dividends for the company or owner, but the development of every branch of the business to its highest state of excellence, so that the **prosperity may be permanent.**"* [1]

With the publication of his work called *The Principles of Scientific Management* in 1911, Frederick W. Taylor clarified that the primary objective of a profit-oriented organization, its management, and its shareholders are the same and it is to secure the creation of maximum and permanent prosperity which has been redefined as the creation of maximum shareholder value and sustainable profitability for further clarity in the early 1960s. In the book of Milton Friedman entitled *Capitalism and Freedom,* first published in 1962, he explained the social responsibility of a business or profit-oriented organization as follows *"there is one and only one social responsibility of business—to use its resources and engage in activities designed to increase its profits so long as it stays within the rules of the game, which is to say, engages in open and free competition without deception or fraud."*[2]

Since then, the creation of maximum shareholder value and sustainable profitability has been widely accepted as the *primary objective and performance measure* of executives and the business organization they run on behalf of its shareholders because it is specific, measurable, assignable, realistic, time-bound, and aligned with the primary objective of the shareholders in financing their business. And while to secure the creation of maximum shareholder value and sustainable profitability is not codified in statute to manage a profit-oriented organization, the court affirm this primary objective too but subject to *business judgment rule* which means the court will presume that the Board of Directors or management act on an informed basis or in honest belief that their business decisions are in the best interest of the corporation although those decisions may result to loss of economic opportunities or business failure due to the inherent difficulty to predict the future with certainty.

Looking back at the history of business management, we can find that the search of *one best way* to do work or to manage a business started by Frederick W. Taylor has been influential in the development of management as a profession and in the economic progress that we have achieved in the last hundred years. Because as we seek to secure the creation of maximum shareholder value and sustainable profitability in the economy in the passage of time and change in the economic environment, we keep on developing products, services, and methods to do work or to manage a business (e.g. strategy, business model, organizational design, and methods of business operation) to help executives and the business organizations they run to secure it. As a result, we have reached a tremendous level of efficiency and productivity in our business organizations using the one best way to do work or the so-called best management practices that include the science of work (Time and motion study) and its further improvement (e.g. Mass Production, Toyota Production System, Value Chain, and Reengineering). However, as we achieved the massive efficiency and productivity using better methods and advanced technologies, our global economy has been shifted from make-to-order to make-to-stock or service-on-demand that give us the power and freedom to choose from numerous products and services that come from various suppliers around the world. And as the number of choices has increased and the free market capitalism has been adopted to run the world economy, a second era of competition has been created herein called *the age of borderless competitions and numerous alternative products as shown in Figure 1.*

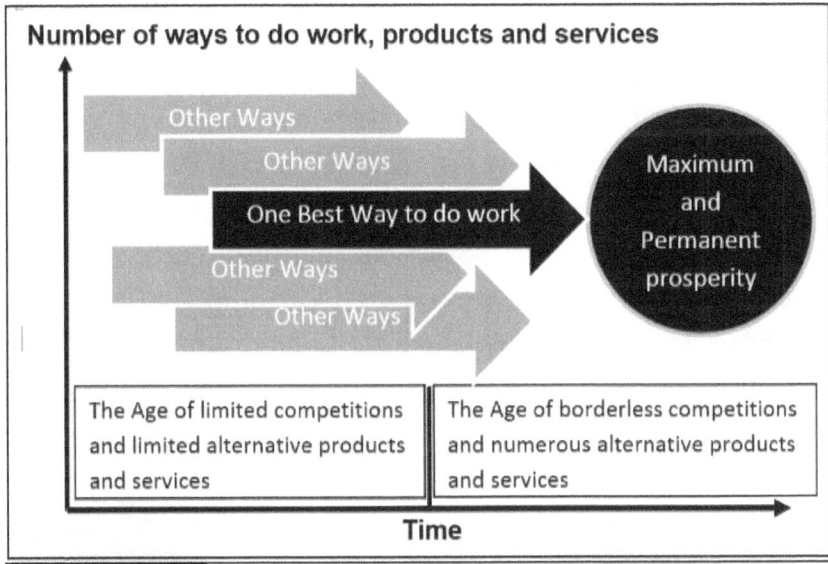

Figure 1 — Wealth creation as catalyst of progress

As we seek to create wealth to protect our interest or welfare in the global economy, we keep on inventing numerous products, services, and methods to do work or to manage a business that have transformed our economy and way of life. As result, a second era of competition was born herein called the age of borderless competitions and numerous alternative products.

This economic environment is significantly different from the time the principles of scientific management were developed by Frederick W. Taylor wherein the competitions and the existing alternative products and services were both limited due to the economic, political, and technological barriers that exist on that time (e.g. lack of efficient method of production, advanced machineries, efficient mode of mass communication, free trade agreements, modern packaging, and mass transportation). In the new era, we can observe that the competition become so stiff and is taking place almost everywhere and in everything. As a result, many business organizations that cannot adopt or compete in the second era of competition failed or simply disappeared despite of its success to secure the creation of significant shareholder value and profit for many decades in the past (e.g. Sears, Toys R Us, Penn Central Transportation Company, Kodak, Blockbuster, and Circuit City). Some were sold for survival (e.g. Chrysler, Yahoo, Mitsubishi Motors, Nissan, Sun Microsystem, Motorola Mobility, and Nokia Mobile devices and services division) and some have just stopped growing and now on the path of total obsolescence (e.g. Western Union, Xerox, Toshiba, and Blackberry). And with the increasing number of failure among previously successful companies in the past, we can observe that we are brought back to the century-old question: What is the *One Best Way* to do work or to manage a business to secure the creation of maximum shareholder value and sustainable profitability in the passage of time and change in the economic environment? With the publication of *The Principles of Scientific Management* in 1911, Frederick W. Taylor thought he found the answer but today we are still asking the question.

Objective Myopia

The creation of maximum shareholder value and sustainable profitability has been widely considered as the primary objective and performance measure of executives and the business organization they run on behalf of its shareholders around the world and yet many executives' understandings of the primary objective can be observed myopic. What has been understood myopically by many executives is the primary objective of the shareholders for which they financed the company: To secure the creation of maximum shareholder value and sustainable profitability *regardless* of the product, service, business, industry or market the company may operate in the passage of time and change in the economic environment as long as the primary objective will be legally achieved. Why?

Because from the economic perspective of the shareholders, to secure the maximum return on capital or to make money as much as possible (which is achieved when the public corporation secure the creation of maximum shareholder value and sustainable profitability) is their primary objective because as we have shifted the global economy from barter to the use of currency, we are rich or poor according to the degree in which we can afford to enjoy the necessaries, conveniences, and amusements of human life using money. These perspectives are supported by many known economists, executives, and management consultants too. For instance, in one of the famous New York Times articles in 1970, Milton Friedman explained the direct responsibility of the executives to its employers as well as the primary objective of the shareholders in his own words

*"In a free-enterprise, private-property system, a corporate executive is an employee of the owners of the business. He has direct responsibility to his employers. That responsibility is to conduct the business in accordance with their desires, which generally will be **to make as much money as possible** while conforming to the basic rules of the society, both those embodied in law and those embodied in ethical custom."*[3]

And from the history of business management, Alfred Sloan Jr., the legendary CEO of General Motors, explained the primary objective of the company as follows

*"The strategic aim of business is **to earn a return on capital**, and if in any particular case the return in the long run is not satisfactory, then the deficiency should be corrected, or the activity abandoned for a more favorable one."*[4]

Jack Welch, who achieved the creation of more than $400 billion shareholders' value and decades of profitability that earned him the title as the Manager of the 20th Century, viewed the shareholders' primary objective and his duty as the Chairman and CEO of General Electric in the same way like Milton Friedman, and Alfred Sloan Jr., which is to secure the creation of maximum shareholder value and sustainable profitability regardless of the product, service, business, industry or market GE may operate as long as its primary objective will be achieved. It is the reason why he scans the market and enters on a business that offer an economic opportunity to make money as close to low hanging fruit. He exits from a particular business too (regardless of its performance in the past) if commoditization is taking place and GE does not have the competitive advantage to win.[5]

Steve Jobs, who allocated Apple's resources to reinvent the products and services of other industries (e.g. music player, phone, online stores, and games) after accepting his defeat in personal computer, receives no complaint but praise from Apple's shareholders and Wall Streeters as he led the company to become the world's largest public companies by market capitalization and among the most profitable public companies in the last decade.

Frederick W. Taylor, the father of Scientific Management, expressed the same economic view too when he defined that the principal object of the management or the primary objective of a business organization and its shareholders which is to secure the creation of maximum and permanent prosperity without associating the primary objective of a company to a particular product, service, business, industry or market where it should operate.

Warren Buffett's clear understanding of the primary objective of the shareholders in financing a company can be observed from the way he allocates Berkshire Hathaway's capital in various companies that operate in different products, services, businesses, industries or markets using the return on investment as guide. It is for the same reason he moves the company's capital to other investment alternative when he perceives that the economic opportunity to make money has changed or will be unfavorable in the foreseeable future. The clarity of his understanding of the primary objective of the company and its shareholders can be easily validated too from the rules he established to manage a business as follows:

Rule No. 1: Never lose money.

Rule No. 2: Never forget rule number 1.

However, due to the myopic understanding of many executives on the primary objective of the shareholders on the business organizations they run, they are allocating its capital within a specific product, service, business, industry or market they are in or they believe they know which is limiting the economic opportunity of the company and can be viewed to be far from the primary objective of the shareholders which is to achieve the maximum return on investment or to make money as much as possible *regardless* of the product, service, business, industry or market the company may operate in the passage of time and change in the economic environment as long as the primary objective will be legally achieved. The gap in the view of the primary objective exists because from the perspective of managing a company, the executives of multi-million or billion US dollar companies, for instance, can easily expand its organizational capabilities by simply hiring someone with expertise to understand the emerging economic opportunities brought by transformative products, services, or methods to do work or to manage a business to seize it like how George Westinghouse bought the patents of Nikola Tesla related to electric generators, transformers, and AC motors and then hired him as a technical consultant that ushered us to the age of electricity and help Westinghouse Electric Corporation to make huge money.

But due to the executives' objective myopia, we can observe that many companies and its shareholders had been deprived of some of the biggest economic opportunities to make money from numerous companies with transformative products, services, or methods to do work that emerged in the world economy outside the industry that the executives know or they are in to the extent that the company under their management soon failed, stopped growing, or was sold for survival when its products or services became obsolete or the source of the company's livelihood was taken away by the same startup or existing companies that the executives previously ignored (e.g. Railroad companies failed when its executives ignored the automobile and airline companies, Western Union missed the great economic opportunity to make money when it ignored the impact of patent of Alexander Graham Bell, and Yahoo failed when it ignored the impact of Google's search engine technology).

To quantify the amount of economic opportunities lost by numerous companies and its shareholders due to its executives' own objective myopia, we will go back on the history when the personal computer, the internet, and the smartphone were about to revolutionize and transform our economy and way of life starting in the early 1970s that continue until today. By looking back at this particular period, we can find and conclude that many executives of business organizations that achieved the creation of significant amount of shareholder value and decades of profitability before the arrival of the *Information Age* had failed to allocate its capital (e.g. as low as $35 million US dollar of cash) that had caused their companies and its shareholders to miss some of the biggest economic opportunities to secure the creation of significant amount of shareholder value and profit in the field of information technology that have been dominated by startup companies like Microsoft, Apple, Intel, Dell, Oracle, Adobe, Yahoo, eBay, Amazon, Google, Alibaba, LinkedIn, Tencent and Facebook as well as by Venture Capital companies in the like of Sequoia, KPCB, Naspers, and Softbank at different period in the last fifty years. The amount of economic opportunities missed by many large companies and its shareholders due to executives' own objective myopia is staggering and can be measured through several publications. For instance, Sequoia Capital, founded in 1972 by Donald T. Valentine, invested few million US dollars on several startup companies in the field of information technology such as Atari, Apple, Yahoo, Cisco and other technology companies that on a particular period of time had created a total market capitalization around 1.4 trillion US dollars.[6] And at the start of internet revolutions in the early 1990s, Kleiner, Perkins, Caufield and Byers (KPCB) and Sequoia Capital invested twelve million and five hundred thousand US dollars each at Google (founded in 1998) that turned into 3 to 4 billion US dollars return on their investment when Google went Public in 2004.[7] Masayoshi Son of Softbank of Japan invested around $20 million US dollars on Alibaba (founded by Jack Ma in 1999 in China) that turned to more than $90 billion US dollars within a particular period after Alibaba went Public in 2014. The return of Softbank's investment was equivalent to

4,500 times from the company's original investment which is considered as an astronomical achievement for an executive who is primarily responsible to secure the creation of maximum shareholder value and sustainable profitability on which the executives' performance is measured.[8] Naspers, a little-known publishing company from South Africa, invested 32 million US dollar in the early days of Tencent in 2001 that was translated to USD 175 Billion market value in 17 years while many century-old media and publishing companies around the world had been struggling to find ways to make money in the *Information Age*.[9] And from the study and analysis of the history as we search for one best way to do work or to manage a business in the last hundred years, we can find that many executives missed to make money too by failing to invest on the second wave of business transformation of an existing public company like Apple that created more than one trillion US dollar of market value and became one of the most profitable companies in the recent history with the reinvention of music player, online stores, mobile computing, games, and telephone. But if we will go back on the history of business management as early 20th Century, not all executives missed to invest on emerging economic opportunities from an established company. In 1914 for instance, the Executives of the already profitable chemical company called Du Pont invested few million US dollars in General Motors that was soon translated to several billion US dollars that can be considered as one of the biggest pay off in corporate investment in the early 20th Century.[10] And to measure further the great economic opportunities missed by numerous executives to make money in the information technology due to their own objective myopia, in the *Global Top 100 companies by Market Capitalization* compiled by PWC as of March 31, 2018, seven out of top ten largest companies by market capitalizations in the world are all technology companies that did not exist fifty years ago. The seven information technology companies have recorded a combined market capitalization around USD 4.4 trillion US dollars led by Apple (USD 851B), Alphabet (USD 719B), Microsoft (USD 703B), Amazon (701B), Tencent (USD 496B), Alibaba (USD 470B) and Facebook (USD 464B).[11]

Many Board of Directors of Fortune 1000 were sleeping at work from the view of Don Valentine as many big companies, including Xerox, missed the great economic opportunities to make money from information technology companies at Silicon Valley.[12] However, despite of the huge economic opportunities missed by many companies and its shareholders due to executives' own objective myopia, we can observe that there is no discussion or call to bring out and address this management issue related to the allocation of capital. In the research paper called *The Theory of Firm: Managerial Behavior, Agency Costs and Ownership Structure*, Michael C. Jensen and William H. Meckling observed and wrote the following:

"Indeed, it is likely that the most important conflict arises from the fact that as the manager's ownership claim falls, his incentive to devote significant effort to creative activities such as searching out new profitable ventures falls. He may in fact avoid such ventures simply because it requires too

much trouble or effort on his part to manage or to learn about new technologies. Avoidance of these personal costs and the anxieties that go with them also represent a source of on-the-job utility to him and it can result in the value of the firm being substantially lower than it otherwise could be."[13]

The great economic opportunity to make money missed by numerous executives in the advent of personal computer, internet, and smartphone revolutions can be gleaned as well from the view of John Sculley, the former CEO of Apple and Pepsi, when he said in his own words

"Healthcare missed the PC and Internet revolutions, but it can't afford to miss the cloud and mobile revolution." [14]

However, from the history of business management in the last hundred years, we can find that it is not only the healthcare companies in the like of Pfizer and GlaxoSmithKline that missed the huge economic opportunities brought by information technology because the cash-rich Oil & Gas companies in the like of ExxonMobil, BP, Chevron, Total, Aramco and Shell had missed it too (while ExxonMobil tried to enter in Personal Computer business in the 1980s, it failed to acquire or invest on startup companies like Apple, Intel, Oracle, and Microsoft). The executives of giant telecom companies such as AT&T and Verizon can be observed to miss the same great economic opportunities too despite they were sitting with several billions of cash or capital. The executives of automobile industry (e.g. General Motors and Ford), the airline companies (e.g. Boeing and United Airlines) and the century-old business organizations like Procter & Gamble, Nestle and Coca-Cola can be observed to miss the same great economic opportunities despite their executives can easily participate on numerous startup companies with transformative products, services, and methods to do work or to manage a business by investing or acquiring the startup companies that emerged in the early 1970s onwards via a Corporate Venture Capital Arm in the same way Sequoia, Softbank, Naspers and KPCB did. From the history, we can observe that there are too many business organizations and shareholders around the world that had been deprived by some of the biggest economic opportunities to make money from information technology not because of lack of capital or because of the absence of economic opportunity to grow rather there was a failure of management, primarily in the allocation of capital, due to its executives' own objective myopia. And while the failure of management in the allocation of capital is widespread and the amount of economic opportunities missed was so huge amounting to several billion to trillion US dollars as illustrated, no executives came forward to accept their failure of management, primarily in the allocation of capital, except to Warren Buffett, the CEO of Berkshire Hathaway. In one of the Berkshire Hathaway shareholders' meeting, Warren Buffett personally admitted to his shareholders that he missed to invest in companies like Google and Amazon because he failed to understand how Google will make money and under estimated the capabilities of Jeff Bezos to executes his strategy.[15] With the outstanding performance of Warren Buffett to produce a remarkable return on Berkshire Hathaway's capital under his management, no shareholders have the guts to ask him about his failure in the allocation of capital. However, despite of his outstanding investment performance, Warren Buffett came forward and publicly acknowledged his failure in the allocation of capital because he knew deep inside that his duty as an executive of the company he run on behalf of its shareholders is to secure the creation of maximum return on capital and from what has been taking place in the information technology industry where Venture Capital companies are thriving is too big to ignore. Hence, he made his adjustment in his investment methodology by investing in technology companies and startup companies too which he claimed that he does not understand before. And with his admission on his shortcomings as the Chairman and CEO of Berkshire Hathaway, the Oracle of Omaha showed that he was not only one of the greatest investors in history but one of the most ethical and transparent executives of a public company in history too.

If we will look back at the history, the objective myopia among many executives has existed for more than a century but left undiscussed if we will trace it starting from the railroad and telegraph companies in the mid-19th Century. From the history as we search to find the one best way to do work or to manage a business in the last hundred years, we can find that it is being repeated throughout the history. For instance, the manufacturers of typewriter soon found themselves to be thoroughly massacred by numerous Personal Computer companies in the advent of information technology in the same way how the automobile killed the horse breeding companies and made the highly successful railroad business unprofitable. Yahoo was sold for survival when its executives failed to buy Google's search engine technology in the early days similar to the failure of Western Union's executives to buy the telephone patent of Alexander Graham Bell. These kinds of events can be observed repeated again when the discount store, internet, and outsourcing companies took the world economy by storm at different period in the last hundred years that caught many executives unprepared. The consequence? Many successful business organizations in the past soon failed or simply disappeared. Some were sold for survival and some simply have stopped growing and now on the path of total obsolescence but not because of lack of capital to enter in emerging business with transformative products, services, and methods to do work or because of the absence of economic opportunities in the market to grow rather there was a failure from its management, primarily in the allocation of capital, due to its executives' own objective myopia.

A failure of management from the top

The failure of management in the allocation of capital comes from the top. The root cause of the failure of many companies to secure the creation of maximum shareholder value and sustainable profitability in the passage of time and change in the economic environment can be traced to its Board of Directors and Chief Executive Officer's own objective myopia. They focus on the business within the industry they are in or they believed they know which is limiting the economic opportunity of the company. As a consequence, they missed some of the biggest economic opportunities to make money from the arrival of numerous transformative products, services, and methods to do work despite the company is sitting with huge amount of capital to the extent that the company under their management soon failed, stopped growing or ended up being sold for survival not because of lack of capital to enter in the emerging business or because of the absence of economic opportunities to grow rather there has been a failure of management, primarily in the allocation of capital due to executives own objective myopia. Thus:

The railroad companies

The railroad companies that achieved the creation of significant shareholder value and decades of profitability for many years in the mid-19th Century due to its breakthrough technology and unmatched availability of its transportation service in all-weather condition soon failed not because of lack of capital to enter in emerging business that have transformative products, services, and methods to do work or because of the absence of economic opportunities in the market to grow rather there was a failure from its management, primarily in the allocation of its capital, due to its executives' own objective myopia. Why? Because from 1870 to 1970 which is designated as the special century,[16] the United States of America had been an exciting place to grow and make enormous money due to the invention of numerous transformative products, services, and methods to do work or to manage a business that could have provided the railroad companies the necessary economic opportunities to secure the creation of maximum shareholder value and sustainable profitability starting from the invention of practical telephone in 1876, the invention of the practical light bulb in 1879, the invention of induction motor in 1887 (and AC generator and transformer that ushered us to the *Age of electricity*), the arrival of Oil Age (starting from the invention of Kerosene as alternative to candle in 1859 followed by the invention of the gasoline-powered automobile in 1885, and then the invention of plastic in 1907), the invention of motion picture camera in 1892 (that created the entertainment industry), the invention of radio in 1895 (that created the mass advertising industry), the invention of air conditioning unit in 1902, the invention of airplane in 1903, the mass production of automobile in 1913, the invention of practical television in 1927, the establishment of discount stores in 1962 (later dominated by Walmart), and the advent of information age starting from the early 1970s that continue until today. From the history of business management, we can observe that the previous success of the railroad companies had caused their executives to believe that it was the railroad business they were good at and attribute their company's success to their expertise. Hence, they failed to organize their company around its primary objective and failed to expand their organizational capabilities to understand the various emerging transformative products, services, and methods to do work invented by various individuals or companies across different industries in the passage of time and change in the economic environment to be able to allocate its capital efficiently and effectively and seize the glaring economic opportunities either through merger and acquisition, investment, joint venture, patent acquisition, franchising, cross licensing agreement or even hiring the genius behind the transformative product, service, or method to do work either as an employee or management consultant. By the time the railroad executives recognized their management deficiencies and attempted to diversify their train transportation company, it was too late to save their company from bankruptcy.

Western Union

After creating significant shareholder value and profit for many decades in the past because of its breakthrough technology, Western Union founded in 1851 soon stopped growing as the company's cutting edge telegraph technology was replaced by the invention of the telephone in 1876 and then followed by the internet in the late 1960s that soon powered by easy to use World Wide Web by 1989 that have changed the way we communicate and access information completely. As a consequence, Western Union sent its last telegram in 2006 to mark the end of an era. And while the company's core business was made obsolete by more advanced technologies, Western Union was survived by its venture on money transfer business where it is still holding a significant market shares around the world today. However, while the company is one of the major players in money transfer business, we can observe that it may be facing its biggest challenge to thwart the risk of obsolescence on its entire corporate history as the last bastion of its business, the money transfer, is the prime target for disruption by many large technology companies like Apple, Google, Facebook, Samsung, Alibaba and many startup Fintech companies funded by Venture Capital and Private Equity companies. And when the money transfer business will be reinvented, no one may remember that Western Union was once a shaper of American corporate history. More than a century earlier, Western Union emerged as one of the largest and most powerful companies in United States of America and the world. By 1866 for instance, Western Union had seized the control of the largest telegraph network in America, becoming the first American private corporation to monopolize a national industry. The market shares of its telegraph business in the United States of America reached 90 percent.[17] Yet, the company soon failed to sustain its growth and maintain its relevance in the business of information and communication due to its executives' own objective myopia. Throughout the Western Union's history while the company had been sitting with large amount of cash or capital brought by the superiority of its telegraph technology, the executives of Western Union had believed that it was the business of telegraph they were good at or the industry that they know that soon deprived their business organization and its shareholders to make money on emerging companies that have transformative products, services, and methods to do work or to manage a business in the last hundred years that could have provided Western Union the means to secure the creation of maximum shareholder value and sustainable profitability in the passage of time and change in the economic environment. And due to the failure of its executives to expand its organizational capabilities to understand the telephone technology, they failed to buy the telephone patent of Alexander Graham Bell which was offered to them for just $100,000 dollars. The failure of executives of Western Union to understand the impact of telephone in the societies and the world economy had caused their company and its shareholder to miss one of the biggest economic opportunities that was created by a single transformative technology, the telephone. To mention, AT&T was so successful to the extent it was dismantled into several companies by US government as part of its anti-trust move to protect the American consumers from monopoly. And from the study and analysis of the history of business management in the last hundred years, we can find that Western Union had missed the numerous great economic opportunities inside and outside its industry in the passage of time and change in the economic environment not because of lack of capital to enter in emerging business with transformative products, services, and methods to do work or because of the absence of economic opportunities in the market to grow rather, like the railroad companies, there was a failure from its management, primarily in the allocation of capital, due to its executives' own objective myopia.

The five powerful but myopic perspectives used by executives to run a business organization

It is impossible to have a widespread failure of management in the allocation of capital that would be left undetected for more than a century without a cause. Hence, we will discuss the five powerful but inherently myopic perspectives that have been widely accepted and used by many executives as a rule of thumb to run a business organization because of its proven power to create a significant amount of shareholder value and profit in the past. These five perspectives have been identified and codified from personal accounts of many successful entrepreneurs and from the various studies conducted on many successful companies and its executives as we search to find the *one best way* to do work or to manage a business in the last hundred years. And from the study and analysis of the history of the development of best management practices, we can find that the failure of management in the allocation of capital remained undetected and left undiscussed because the duration of the success of many companies that used these five powerful perspectives was so long to the extent that its obscured the fact to the next generation of executives and shareholders that the perspectives that had been used by executives to succeed had caused their company to miss some of the biggest economic opportunities to make money that emerged in the economy and had put their business organization on the path of total obsolescence in the passage of time and change in the economic environment. The five powerful but inherently myopic perspectives use by many executives as a rule of thumb are as follows:

Perspective 1: Do what you love, love what you do, and never give up.

Perspective 2: We should broadly define our business around the customers' needs within the industry we are in to sustain its profitability or growth.

Perspective 3: Stick to the knitting or invest in the business that you know.

Perspective 4: Put all your eggs in one basket and then watch that basket.

Perspective 5: Focus on your core business or core competency.

Each of these five powerful but inherently myopic perspectives to run a business organization will be discussed in detail to explain how the erroneous use of these perspectives can lead to executives' own objective myopia that will soon prevent a company to secure the creation of maximum shareholder value and sustainable profitability in the passage of time and change in the economic environment.

Perspective 1: *Do what you love, love what you do, and never give up.*

Doing what you love and build your business around it is a very powerful perspective to manage a business especially when starting from scratch. Louis V. Gerstner Jr., who save IBM from its near-death experience, considered the need to know and love the business as one of the important lessons he learned at IBM.[18] And we learned the power of this perspective as well through personal accounts of many highly successful executives who started from scratch and we are lucky at their openness to share their own experience through books, magazines, news, and internet. They honestly tell us that if you follow your heart and turn your passion into business, success will follow especially if you don't give up. Hence, this perspective has been widely accepted and used by many executives and entrepreneurs around the world as a rule of thumb to start or manage a business.

However, despite of its wisdom and power to achieve success in business, many executives and entrepreneurs who use this powerful perspective in the long run have created their own objective myopia. Because as executives or entrepreneurs use their passion to run their business organization, they ignored some of the biggest economic opportunities that emerged in other industries because it is far from what they love to do. As a consequence, they deprived their company and its shareholders on some of the biggest economic opportunities to make money from other industries to the extent that they ended up serving their own interest by doing only what they love to do and not the interest of the company and its shareholders whose primary objective is to secure the creation of maximum shareholder value and sustainable profitability regardless of the product, service, business, industry or market their company may operate in the passage of time and change in the economic environment as long as the primary objective will be legally achieved. And while we may find absurd if the executives ignore the economic opportunities that can offer to make money as close to low hanging fruit or that can offer huge return on investment like in the case of startup technology companies that started in the early 1970s, many executives ignored it because it was far from the business they love to do that can explain the reason why many executives of century-old business organizations (e.g. Pharmaceutical, Oil & Gas, FMCG, Automobile, Telecommunications and many other large corporations) failed to participate in the Personal Computer, Internet, and Smartphone revolutions and lost more than hundred billions of economic opportunities to make money out of thirty two million US dollar or less of investment despite of the fact that they were sitting with several billions of cash. For some companies, the consequence is costly when the source of its livelihood is taken away by the same startup companies its executives had previously ignored (e.g. Sears on ignoring the arrival of Amazon or Blockbuster on ignoring Netflix).

Perspective 2: *We should broadly define our business around the customers' needs within the industry we are in to sustain its profitability or growth.*

In 1960, prior to the age of borderless competitions and numerous alternative products, Theodore Levitt wrote his Harvard Business Review Article called *Marketing Myopia* that inspired many executives to have serious thought about one of the famous questions in management: *"What business are you really in?"* The question is derived from Theodore Levitt's analysis on the observed failure of the railroad companies to sustain its growth despite the population grew as observed by Harry Igor Ansoff in his HBR article called *Strategies for Diversification* in 1957. In Marketing Myopia, Theodore Levitt argued that:

"had the railroad executives seen themselves as being in the transportation business rather than in the railroad business, they would have continued to grow."[19]

True. Because from the perspective of managing a business, viewing the railroad business to transportation business which include cars, trucks, and airplane offered a powerful insight how the railroad executives could have sustained its profitability or growth. As a result, it has been widely used by many executives that operate in different industries to manage their business organizations. However, despite of its powerful insight, if we will study and analyze the history of business management in the last hundred years, we can find that this perspective is true only in the short run and not true in the long run because less than sixty years from the date of the publication of Marketing Myopia, we can find that if the executives of the railroad companies could have viewed its railroad business correctly to transportation business (which include cars, trucks, and airplanes), it grew but they ended up on the same fate like the railroad that pleaded for government subsidies to survive due to the fact that the US government have to bail out the American automobile and airline companies at different period within the last sixty years. To discuss the numerous events that took place in the American transportation industry, we can learn from the history that by the year 2001, the already ailing airline industry of the United States of America received bailout packages amounting to several billions of US dollars from American government to save the entire industry from devastating effect of terrorist attack on September 11, 2001.[20] And by the year 2009, the American automobile companies such as General Motors and Chrysler received billions of dollars in the form of bailout funds from the US government. Similarly, Ford Motor Company received billions of dollars support from US government in the form of business loan[21] and Boeing, the American export powerhouse, received billions of US dollars too in the form of guaranteed credit line from the US Export-Import Bank, an American government bank.[22] These direct and indirect financial assistance from US government were deemed necessary so that the American airlines and American automobile industries can survive the havoc effect of 2001 and 2008 crises that threatened even the existence of some of the oldest and largest companies in United States of

America. The US government intervention can be observed far from the free market policy which the US had championed in the past decades, but the financial support was necessary accordingly to save millions of American jobs. *Too big to fail* was the term coined to justify the government intervention to save the various private companies that operate in different industries to minimize the catastrophic effect of 2008 financial crisis in the American societies and the world economy. From the study of the history, we can find that without the financial support from the US government at different period, the railroad, the airlines, and the automobiles companies of America (including some of the biggest financial institutions) will not be around today even the executives of the railroad companies could have broadened correctly its business within the transportation industry in accordance with the analysis of Theodore Levitt in Marketing Myopia. Hence, we can learn and conclude that expanding within the industry we are in can be observed to be myopic too in relation to the objective of the executives and the business organization they run to secure the creation of maximum shareholder value and sustainable profitability. Moreover, we can find that to view the railroad business within the transportation business only, the railroad companies and its shareholders missed some of the biggest economic opportunities amounting to hundreds of billion to more than a trillion US dollars that emerged from different industries in the world economy in the passage of time and change in the economic environment like the telephone, PC, and internet.   From the study and analysis of the history of development of transformative products, services, and methods to do work, the railroad executives could have done better if they understood correctly the primary objective of the business organization they run for which it is established and financed by its shareholders which is to secure the creation of maximum shareholder value and sustainable profitability *regardless* of the products, services, business, industry, or market they may operate in the passage of time and change in the economic environment as long as the primary objective for which the company is financed by its shareholders will be legally achieved. Had they understood correctly the primary objective of the shareholders, we can expect that they will organize their company around the emerging business with transformative technologies that offer some of the biggest economic opportunities to grow and they will improve as well their organizational capabilities to understand completely the numerous transformative products, services, and methods to do work that emerged from the early 1870s onwards (e.g. light bulb, electric generation and distribution, antibiotics, radio, television etc.) so that they can allocate their capital efficiently and effectively on numerous companies that shaped our economy and way of life in the last hundred years. Furthermore, had they understood the primary objective of their company correctly, we could expect them to be in the car, airplane, and telephone business too among others through their constant watchfulness on the arrival of economic opportunities brought by these transformative products, services, and methods to do work or to manage a business. And as the economic opportunity change in the passage of time and change in the economic environment, we could expect them to be out from any of these businesses at the time that these products and services are being commoditized or facing obsolescence and do not represent the best use of its capital within the foreseeable future. From the study of the history, we can observe that due to the widespread acceptance of analyzing the business within the industry we are in, many executives view their competitions within the industry too as if the boundary of economic competitions is within the given industry only. To illustrate the effect of executives' myopic view of competition at industry level, many executives of companies typically do not consider the banks, real estate, and automobile as their competitors and yet every company compete on disposable income of consumers in the economy based on the hierarchy of their needs. For instance, when a customer bought a house and automobile on credit and then mortgage the same in a bank, his disposable income is significantly reduced by the monthly installment of loans that include the profits of the bank, the profit of real estate developer, and the profit of automobile manufacturer and dealer. And as the borrower must legally meet his monthly commitment, he must reduce his spending somewhere else in the economy such as reducing the frequency to eat in fancy restaurants, to buy branded clothes, or to visit hotels for a weekend holiday. The effect of the limited disposable income and the hierarchy of needs that can affect a company to sell its product was realized by Bill Gates on his visit in one poor area in Africa to demonstrate the power of computer to the kids in line with Microsoft's vision to have 'computer on every desk and in every home'. The ground experience of Bill Gates has changed his view because he found that he needed to borrow a generator before he can start the computer presentation using Windows Operating System and Microsoft Office that his company developed. Like many technology executives today who dream to connect every individual in the world in the internet, Bill Gates changed his perspectives due to his ground experience. He found that there is hierarchy of needs that need to be address first before connecting the seven billion people around the world and the hierarchy of needs is a fact that affect the business which we cannot ignore.[23] Perhaps, the same blunder took place among companies in the horse breeding industry. While the executives of the largest breeders of horses were busy analyzing its competitors and mapping their business strategy on how they can increase their market share and improve the breed of their horses, the executives of the automobiles, like Henry Ford and Alfred Sloan Jr., were plotting their obsolescence that soon kill their business. Today, without the ultra-rich or royal families' passion on equestrian as their sports, the horse may be seen only in the zoo for educational purposes.

Perspective 3: *Stick to the knitting or invest in the business that you know.*

In 2018 Berkshire Hathaway shareholder meeting, Warren Buffett, the Oracle of Omaha, personally admitted that he was wrong for not investing on Google and Amazon. To mention what he missed, both technology companies are among the top five companies with the largest market capitalization in the world that did not exist less than 30 years ago. Google's money-making machine is so powerful that it makes money every time someone click on the text ads shown along with the result of the most popular search engine in the world. In the case of Amazon, the company has transformed the business of bookstore, retail industry, movies, and cloud computing in unprecedented way that made the company to become the second American public company to achieve more than one trillion US dollar market capitalization that catapulted Jeff Bezos, its founder, to become the richest man on the planet. While Berkshire Hathaway's shareholders did not ask why he failed to invest in Google and Amazon, Warren Buffett admitted his failure of management in the allocation of the company's capital to seize one of the biggest economic opportunities to make money that emerged in the world economy. He described the source of his failure by stating the following in his own words

"I made the mistake in not being able to come to a conclusion where I really felt that at the present prices that the prospects were far better than the prices indicated."[24]

And given the Berkshire Hathaway's rising market value that generated 20.9 percent annual return from 1965 to 2017 compared to S&P 500 of 9.9 percent, Warren Buffett's performance earned him as one of the most successful investors in history. Hence, we may be asking why he is apologizing to his investors and what is the factor that caused the great Oracle of Omaha to miss some of the biggest economic opportunities to make money in companies like Google and Amazon at the beginning of internet revolution?

To understand the management perspective that caused Warren Buffett's failure to invest in technology companies, it is necessary to study the history to understand how he invest. In 1974 Forbes staff asked Warren Buffett to give general suggestions on investing. He replied and stated the following in his own words

*"Above all, **stick with what you know**. Don't get too fancy. Draw a circle around the businesses you understand and then eliminate those that fail to qualify on the basis of value, good management and limited exposure to hard times. No high technology. No multicompanies. I don't understand them."*[25]

Then in 1998, when Warren Buffett was asked why he did not invest on Microsoft or Intel in the early 1980s when PC started to shape our economy and way of life that made Microsoft and Intel to become the two most valuable companies on the planet. His answer is straightforward: he doesn't know enough about the industry.[26]

From the study of the history of business management, we can find that while to stick with what we know or understand is very powerful management perspective that can save you from investment trouble like how Warren Buffett emerged unscathed from dot-com stock bubbles of 2000 and avoided companies like Theranos, the limitation of this perspective is clear: If we will stick with what we know which is inherently limited and don't expand our organizational capabilities to understand the emerging transformative technologies that can shape our economy and way of life in the passage of time and change in the economic environment, we will miss some of the biggest opportunities to make money in the economy because it is impossible to know something that did not exist before. And with close to hundred billion US dollars of capital under Warren Buffett's disposal, to invest thirty two million US dollars or less on startup technology companies that can turn to ninety billion US dollar (like what Softbank achieved on its investment on Alibaba) or one hundred seventy billions US dollars (like what Naspers achieved on its investment on Tencent) is something that he can easily do if he expanded Berkshire Hathaway's organizational capabilities (e.g. by hiring someone with expertise on the subject) to understand the new technologies to be able to allocate the company's capital efficiently and effectively and seize the great economic opportunity to make money. And with more than hundreds of billion to trillion US dollars economic opportunities missed by Berkshire Hathaway and its shareholders in the advent of information technology revolutions due to his perspective to stick with what he knows, he knew that he missed a great economic opportunity. Hence, he believed that it was appropriate that his shareholders to know his shortcomings in the allocation of the company's capital that made him one of the most transparent and ethical executives of our time as discussed.

From the history of business management, it appears that the best time to invest on companies with transformative products, services, and methods to do work or to manage a business rest on its early stage of operation before the company's Initial Public Offering (IPO) because the cost of capital is very low and then hold it for long term perspective. And the key to make money is to have complete understanding of how the new technology will transform the economy and our way of life. This fact is proven by numerous events that took place in the history like the brilliant move by George Westinghouse to buy Nikola Tesla's patents on AC electric generation, transformer, and induction motor that brought us to the *Age of electricity,* the great decision made by Asa Griggs Candler to acquire a formula that built the Coca-Cola empire, and the acquisition of the xerography technology by Haloid Company that ushered us to the age of photocopy that powered the Xerox Corporation to create wealth. These are the kind of investment repeated by Sequoia Capital, Softbank, Naspers, and KPCB in the age information technology but missed by Warren Buffett not because of lack of capital to enter on emerging business or the absence of economic opportunity to grow rather it was due to his perspective to stick with what he knows that deprived Berkshire Hathaway and its shareholders the economic opportunity to make enormous money in the arrival of transformative technologies.

Perspective 4: *Put all your eggs in one basket and then watch that basket*

In the address to the Students of the Curry Commercial College, Pittsburgh, on June 23, 1885, Andrew Carnegie, who will become the richest American sixteen years later after the buyout of his steel company staged by J.P. Morgan in 1901, stated the following advice to the young men in his own words

"And here is the prime condition to success, the great secret: concentrate your energy, thought, and capital exclusively upon the business in which you are engaged. Having begun in one line, to lead in it; adopt every improvement, have the best machinery, and know the most about it." He continued *"The concerns which fail are those which have scattered their*

capital, which means that they have scattered their brains also. They have investments in this, or that, or the other, here, there, and everywhere. 'Don't put all your eggs in one basket' is all wrong. I tell you 'put all your eggs in one basket and then watch that basket'. Look around you and take notice; men who do that do not often fail. It is easy to watch and carry the one basket. It is trying to carry too many baskets that breaks most eggs in this country. He who carries three baskets must put one on his head, which is apt to tumble and trip him up. One fault of the American business man is lack of concentration" [27]

With the achievement of Andrew Carnegie by concentrating his capital in the business of steel, the power of his management perspective to create wealth is accepted as a rule of thumb. Perhaps, there is nothing you need to validate the power of this management perspective if you can succeed to create wealth achieved by Andrew Carnegie throughout your lifetime whose value was equivalent to $372 Billion as of 2014 that made him the richest American has ever lived.[28] Hence, to put all the company's eggs or capital in one basket and watch it diligently is widely used by numerous executives around the world today especially if the company is starting to build its foundation and trying to defend the company's market position.

However, despite of the power and brilliance of this perspective, we can observe that it is true in the short run (especially if you are starting with limited capital) and it can be harmful in the long run if this perspective will stop you to invest and use the accumulated capital on the emerging transformative products, services, or methods to do work or to manage a business that can offer your company to create huge money in the passage of time and change in the economic environment. From the history, we will find that the method to do work of Andrew Carnegie was soon surpassed by Nucor that established mini mill and used recycling of scrap steel as part of the company's strategy starting in 1969. And from the event that took place onwards, the whole American steel industry which hold more than fifty percent of world's production after World War II soon declined as Europe and Japan used more advanced methods of production in the last sixty years that followed. Then came the industrialization in China starting in the 1980s that previously held one third of US production but soon matched it within a decade. Today, half of the steel production in the world is produced in China.[29] Moreover, the United Steel company's market capitalizations and profitability have been eclipsed by numerous companies like the technology companies.

From the study and analysis of the history of management in the last hundred years, we can learn and conclude that every transformative product, service, and method to do work or to manage a business last within a certain period of time. Some inventions or methods to do work last for decades due to its patent and some may last for a century as the company defend it through product development. But no single product can sustain the company's profitability forever because no product or service is immune to commoditization, market saturation, and eventually obsolescence. Why? Because as we seek to create wealth in the economy to protect our own interest or welfare, we keep on inventing and reinventing products, services, and methods to do work or to manage a business that has been shaping continuously the competition and our way of life in the passage of time and change in the economic environment as discussed. Due to this economic fact, the competition in the market is getting stiffer everywhere and in everything that caused many companies to fail, stop growing, or end up being sold for survival as discussed but not because of lack of capital to enter on emerging business with transformative products, services, and methods to do work or because of the absence of economic opportunities to grow rather it is because of the perspective used by many executives like *putting all its eggs in one basket then watching the basket* which, in the final analysis, is inherently myopic that can cause a company to miss some of the biggest economic opportunities that will emerge in the economy and put the company on the path of total obsolescence in the passage of time and change in the economic environment.

Perspective 5: *Focus on your core business and core competencies to sustain the company's profitability or growth*

To manage a business organization and sustain its profitability or growth, executives of companies need to focus on their core business and core competencies. Studies of many successful companies supported the theory that the company's non-core business must be sold. For example, Microsoft sold its travel portal company called expedia.com to focus on its core business for which the company is well known-software development. The result of many management studies also recommends that the non-core activities or functions of a company that do not add value on the product being paid by its customers are better to be outsourced from companies that possessed the relevant capabilities or expertise. For instance, it is better for Microsoft, as a software company, to outsource the maintenance of its facilities than to do by its own. The advantage of this management perspective is very clear: Microsoft and its vendor will gain financial and operational benefits on this kind of arrangement because as the vendor provides the same services to other companies, they can use the power of economies of scale to lower the cost of its services and share the savings back to Microsoft. And in addition to the financial benefits that Microsoft can derived from this arrangement, it is relieved from the hassle of managing the people and the day to day operation to clean and maintain its facilities. Hence, it can focus its energy on its core competencies that produce world class products and services that gives the company the competitive advantage and the means to make enormous money in the world economy. Many Japanese companies used this management perspective to win the competition in the global market too. For instance, Japanese automobile companies surrounded themselves of small and medium companies that manufacture spare parts to bring down the spare parts cost which allow their company to focus on their core business (e.g. manufacturing, assembling, marketing and distributing its automobile around the world) and core competencies (e.g. developing a better materials for the car, developing elegant car designs, and improving the method to engineer and produce a low-cost, high-quality and fuel-efficient car engines). With the numerous benefits that a company can gain by focusing on its core business and core competency, it is not surprising that many executives of business organizations embrace this management perspective as a rule of thumb to manage their business organization.

However, despite of the power of this management perspective, the wrong use of this can lead to executives' own objective myopia because as the executives of company focus on their core business and core competencies for instance, they started to ignore the emerging business that offer some of the biggest economic opportunities to make money in the world economy like in the case of information technology which can pave the way for their company to secure the creation of maximum shareholder value and sustainable profitability in the passage of time and change in the economic environment. For instance, when the executives of numerous companies saw the arrival of Personal Computer powered by Microsoft software and Intel chips, they invested on PCs to achieve efficiency and productivity within their company but many executives did not see the underlying great economic opportunities to make money by investing in Microsoft and Intel which were both positioned to become the industry standard and create enormous wealth as personal computer started to appear in every home and office. The economic opportunities lost by many companies and shareholders can be measured in hundred billion to trillion US dollars as executives focused on their core business and core competencies. And from the study and analysis of the history, the failure of many executives to invest in Microsoft and Intel is not due to lack of capital to invest on emerging technology or the absence of economic opportunities to grow rather there was a failure from its management, primarily in the allocation of capital, due to its executives' own objective myopia. Many executives in different industries had focused on the core business and core competencies as if their business is the only means to earn money or to secure the primary objective of the company in the world economy. But if we will look back on the history in the early 20th Century, we can learn that executives had encountered already a similar event when the automobile was taking the world economy by storm similar to the Personal Computer, internet, and smartphone. But not all executives of business organizations viewed the advent of automobile as a way to achieve efficiency and productivity in their business operations, some executives saw it as a great investment opportunity too. For instance, in the memorandum to Finance Committee of Du Pont Company dated December 19, 1917, Mr. John Raskob, then the Chairman of Finance Committee, called the attention of the Du Pont management to participate in General Motors. He wrote the following in his own words

"The growth of motor business, particularly the General Motors Company, has been phenomenal as indicated by its net earnings and by the fact that the gross receipts of the General Motors-Chevrolet Motor will amount to between $350,000,000.00 and $400,000,000.00. The General Motors

Company today occupies a unique position in the automobile industry and in the opinion of the writer with proper management will show result in the future second to none in any American industry. Mr. Durant perhaps realize this more fully than anyone else and is very desirous of having an organization as perfect as possible to handle this wonderful business."[30]

DuPont's executive management listened on the recommendation of John Raskob and invested 25 million US dollars on December 21, 1917 and then increased it to 49 million US dollar or the equivalent of 28.7 percent of GM common stock at the end of 1919. The result was historical because by the year the Supreme Court ordered Du Pont to divest its GM stock in 1961 due to the perceived conflict of interest related to DuPont paint business with the company, the 63 million GM shares owned by DuPont was worth 2.9 Billion US dollars on that particular time which DuPont divested at different dates after Supreme Court final decision. With the action of DuPont management to enter on emerging business with transformative products, services, and methods to do work or to manage a business like the General Motors at the height of automobile revolutions, we can conclude that there was management failure on the way the Board of Directors, CEOs and CFOs of many business organizations managed their companies, primarily in the allocation of capital, that caused their business organizations and it shareholders to miss the great economic opportunities to make money in the information technology companies like Microsoft and Intel as discussed. And the reason they missed the great economic opportunities to make money in the business of information technology is not because of lack of capital to enter in the emerging business with transformative products, services, and methods to do work or the absence of economic opportunities in the market to grow rather it is because of their management perspective to focus on their core business and core competencies that led its executives to their own objective myopia. And looking back at the history of business management, perhaps, there is no company can match the focus of Kodak on its core business and core competency. Kodak founded by George Eastman in 1888 achieved the creation of significant shareholder value and decades of profitability through its breakthrough product and superior manufacturing capabilities on camera, film, photographic equipment and photo paper. Hence, we can state that the executives' understanding of its core business and core competencies is unquestionable. Kodak's core competency in manufacturing film and photo paper was far superior from its nearest competitor, Fuji film. And aside from Kodak's focus on its core business and core competency, its executives rely heavily on the popularity of its brand and supposed customers' loyalty due to the contribution of Kodak to the society for more than a century. To illustrate the company's focus and intimate relationship with its customers, Kodak was there when we were recording the most significant events in the world history. Kodak was there when people captured the most intimate and most special moments of their lives like when the couple get married, when their first baby was born, and when they celebrate the birthdays of their family members through the years. Kodak was there too when the we celebrated our greatest achievement in life such as winning the Olympic competition or receiving a Nobel Memorial Prize. From Kodak's slogan *"Share moments. Share Life."*, we can state that there is nothing more you can ask for if your company exists to provide the kind of services which Kodak had faithfully provided through the years around the world for more than a century. But looking back at the history of business management, we can find that Kodak executives' focused on its core business and core competency had played a significant role why the company missed some of the biggest economic opportunities to make huge amount of money on the arrival of numerous transformative products, services, and methods to do work or to manage a business in the last century that could have paved the way for Kodak to secure the creation of maximum shareholder value and sustainable profitability in the passage of time and change in the economic environment. Had Kodak used its massive capital to invest or acquire the emerging companies with transformative products, services, or methods to do work, the company could have survived and thrived. But its executives failed to allocate its capital to the extent that they did not even capitalize the digital camera they invented as the company tried to avoid cannibalizing the source of their livelihood. Rather its executives had focused on their core business and core competency that give them competitive advantage in the market in the past until the competitors made their core products obsolete. The company's brand and the expected customers' loyalty due to Kodak's faithful services to its customers in the past did not help for Kodak to survive too. As Japanese companies entered in business areas where Kodak operates with its innovative and easy to use digital cameras, Kodak was not saved by executives' effort to preserve its core business and core competency. It was not saved by its brand and the expected customers' loyalty too which the executives expected from its customers due to the service it has provided in the last hundred years. In January 2012, Kodak filed for Bankruptcy.

In contrast to the sad demise of Kodak, Fujifilm, the second biggest competitor of Kodak for several decades, can be observed to survive and thrive in the age of digital cameras. In the book entitled *Innovating out of Crisis*, Shigetaka Komori tell the inside story of Fujifilm's diversification strategy as he led the company to Healthcare, Cosmetics, Pharmaceutical and many other businesses that have offered Fujifilm the necessary economic opportunities to make money and change its fate very far from Kodak company.[31]

The One Best Way to manage a business to secure the creation of maximum shareholder value and sustainable profitability

If we will study and analyze the history of wealth creation and human intention, we can observe that the invention and reinvention of products, services, and methods to do work are something that we can expect to continue as long as there is human life and free market capitalism is the method that we will use to manage the world economy. Because as we desire to create wealth in the economy to protect our own interest or welfare, we keep on inventing and reinventing products, services, and methods to do work that have transformed continuously our economy and way of life in the passage of time and change in the economic environment (as illustrated in Figure 1). Hence, if we can track and attract the numerous individuals or companies that will invent and reinvent products, services, and methods to do work that can shape our economy and way of life and allocate our capital around it, we will have phenomenal advantage to make money before it become obvious to many (e.g. Sequoia Capital). From the history, many of the inventions and innovations were truly transformative that can be understood. Examples are air conditioners, concrete, elevator, Haber-Bosch Process, penicillin, baby formula, light bulb and computer. And by looking back on the railroad companies that achieved the creation of significant shareholder value and profit in the mid-19th Century due to its transformative technology (e.g. steam engine) and superior service (e.g. all-weather and fast transportation service), we can state and conclude that, had the railroad executives understood correctly the primary objective of the company and its shareholders, they would expand their organizational capabilities beyond what they know or industry they were in to attract the numerous individuals and track the companies that will invent transformative products, services and methods to do work to be able to allocate its capital effectively at different period. Hence, the executives of the railroad companies will be able to sustain its profitability or growth because they will be operating or investing in the business of electric generation and distribution, oil and gas, telecommunication, radio, TV broadcasting, airplane, automobile, air-conditioning, department stores, outsourcing, and information technology as these inventions or innovations are developed by individuals or startup companies around the world at different period. They will continue to monitor and invest on existing public companies too that will reinvent an existing product, service, and method to do work in a revolutionary way like the way Apple reinvent the music player, personal computer, games, and the telephone or the way energy companies improved the fracking technology to extract oil and gas (which the venture capital companies missed because of its focus in information technology and bio-technology only). They will exit too in any of their business units as the product or service become obsolete or being commoditized and they do not possess the competitive advantage to beat the competition like Jack Welch or Warren Buffett did.

References:

1. Frederick Winslow Taylor, *The Principles of Scientific Management* (New York and London: Harper & Brother Publishers, 1919), p. 9.
2. Milton Friedman, *Capitalism and Freedom* (Chicago: The University of Chicago Press, 1962), p. 112.
3. Milton Friedman, *"The Social Responsibility of business is to increase its Profits"*, New York Times Magazine, September 13, 1970
4. Alfred Sloan Jr., *My Years with General Motors* (New York: Doubleday, 1990), p. 49
5. Jack Welch, *Winning* (New York: Harper,2007) p.169.
6. George Anders, "Inside Sequoia Capital: Silicon Valley's Innovation Factory", *Forbes*, March 26,2014, https://www.forbes.com/sites/georgeanders/2014/03/26/inside-sequoia-capital-silicon-valleys-innovation-factory/#df91e793a828 (Accessed May 30, 2015)
7. Matt Marshall, "Did Google Guru make investment ever?", *Siliconbeat 2004*, http://www.siliconbeat.com/entries/2004/11/15/did_google_guru_make_investment_ever.html (accessed October 1, 2017)

8. Peter Elstrom and Pavel Alpeyev, "Softbank's Son Chases Boyhood Dreams with $100 Billion Fund", *Bloomberg 2017*, https://www.bloomberg.com/news/articles/2017-05-21/softbank-s-son-chases-boyhood-dreams-with-100-billion-fund (Accessed: May 22, 2017)
9. Loni Prinsloo, "Tencent's 60,000% Runup Leads to One of the Biggest VC Payoffs Ever", *Bloomberg*, March 3, 2018, https://www.bloomberg.com/news/articles/2018-03-22/naspers-sells-10-6-billion-of-tencent-to-fund-investments (Accessed: July 24, 2018)
10. Phil Frame, "Feds took 15 years to make Du Pont give up stakes at GM", *Automotive News*, June 26, 1996, http://www.autonews.com/article/19960626/ANA/606260744/feds-took-15-years-to-make-dupont-give-up-stake-in-gm (Accessed: September 3, 2017)
11. See "Global Top100 companies by Market Capitalization", *PWC*, March 31, 2018 Update. Page 39.
12. Stanford Graduate School of Business, "Don Valentine, Sequoia Capital: Target Big Markets", YouTube, published October 11, 2010. https://www.youtube.com/watch?v=nKN-abRJMEw (Accessed: December 5, 2018)
13. Michael C. Jensen and William H. Meckling, "Theory of the Firm: Managerial Behavior, Agency Cost and Ownership Structure", *Journal of Financial Economics,* October 1976, V. 3, No. 4, pp. 305-360.
14. https://www.brainyquote.com/quotes/john_sculley_581459 (Accessed May 3 ,2016)
15. Julia Horowitz,"'I blew it': Warren Buffett laments missing out on Google", *CNN Money*, May 6, 2017.http://money.cnn.com/2017/05/06/investing/buffett-google-berkshire-meeting/index.html (Accessed: May 7, 2017).
16. Robert J. Gordon, *The rise and fall of American Growth* (New Jersey: Princeton University Press, 2016), p. 1.
17. Joshua D. Wolff, *Western Union and the creation of the American Corporate Order 1845-1893* (New York: Cambridge Press, 2013, p. 2).

18. Louis V. Gerstner Jr., *Who Says Elephants Can't Dance?* (London: HarperCollinsPublishers, 2002), p.219
19. This analysis is inspired by a discussion in "Marketing Myopia" by Theodore Levitt (Boston: Harvard Business School Publishing Corporation, July-August 2004, p. 138) wherein the cause of failure of the railroad companies can be attributed to executives' product orientation rather than industry orientation due to their own marketing myopia.
20. Michael Arndt, Nanette Byrnes and Lorraine Woellert, "An Airline Bailout -- with Strings Attached", *Bloomberg*, October 8, 2001. https://www.bloomberg.com/news/articles/2001-10-07/an-airline-bailout-with-strings-attached (Accessed: August 12, 2016)
21. Kimberly Amadeo, "Auto Industry Bailout (GM, Ford, Chrysler)", *thebalance.com,* October 3, 2017, https://www.thebalance.com/auto-industry-bailout-gm-ford-chrysler-3305670 (Accessed: January 12, 2018).
22. John Carney, "Boeing Got its Bailout too", *Business Insider*, January 30, 2009, www.businessinsider.com/2009/1/boeing-got-its-bailout-too (Accessed August 12, 2016)
23. Julie Bort, "Bill Gates Talks About the Heartbreaking Moment That Turned Him to Philanthropy", *Business Insider*, January 21, 2015, http://www.businessinsider.com/why-bill-gates-became-a-philanthropist-2015-1#ixzz3bGX41BZv (Accessed May 27, 2015)
24. Alex Crippen and Evely Cheng, "Warren Buffett: I was wrong on Google and too dumb on Amazon", *CNBC 2017*, https://www.cnbc.com/2017/05/06/warren-buffett-admits-he-made-a-mistake-on-google.html (Accessed November 29, 2017)
25. Forber staff, "Warren Buffett – in 1974", *Forbes*, 2008, https://www.forbes.com/2008/04/30/warren-buffett-profile-invest-oped-cx_hs_0430buffett.html#6fbe92cc6759 (Accessed: August 20, 2018)
26. Jeff Pelline, "Buffett won't invest in tech stocks", *CNET 1998*, https://www.cnet.com/news/buffett-wont-invest-in-tech-stocks/ (Accessed July 26, 2016)
27. Andrew Carnegie, *The Empire of Business* (New York: Double Day, Page & Co., 1902) p. 17

28. Jacob Davidson, "The 10 richest people of All Time", *Time*, 2015, http://time.com/money/3977798/the-10-richest-people-of-all-time-2/ (Accessed: August 26, 2018)
29. Chris Isidore. "When American Steel was king", *CNN Money*, March 9, 2018, http://money.cnn.com/2018/03/09/news/companies/american-steel-history/index.html?iid=EL (Accessed: June 8, 2018)
30. Alfred Sloan Jr., *My Years with General Motors* (New York: Doubleday, 1990), pp 12-13.
31. Shigetaka Komori, *Innovating Out of Crisis* (California: Stone Bridge Press, 2015)

Marionito C. Marquez is a Certified Public Accountant and a former Auditor at Laya Mananghaya & Co. (now KPMG R. Manabat & Co.). He is the author of "The One Best Way to manage a business according to Science." Also available at Amazon.com

www.ingramcontent.com/pod-product-compliance
Lightning Source LLC
Chambersburg PA
CBHW030510220526
45464CB00006B/2737